THE STORY OF
LOUIS VUITTON LUGGAGE

Dedication: For Russ

Published in 2024 by OH
An imprint of Welbeck Non-Fiction Limited, part of Welbeck Publishing Group.
Offices in London, 20 Mortimer Street, London W1T 3JW, and Sydney, Level 17,
207 Kent St, Sydney NSW 2000 Australia.
www.welbeckpublishing.com

Text © Laia Farran Graves 2024
Design © Welbeck Non-Fiction Limited 2024
Cover image: Alamy Stock Photo / Pxel

A CIP catalogue record for this book is available from the British Library.

ISBN 978-1-83861-231-3
Publisher: Lisa Dyer
Copy editor: Katie Hewett
Design: Lucy Palmer
Production: Marion Storz

Printed and bound in China

10 9 8 7 6 5 4 3 2 1

THE STORY OF
LOUIS VUITTON LUGGAGE

LAIA FARRAN GRAVES

CONTENTS

INTRODUCTION

The Story of Louis Vuitton Luggage is the tale of one of the most successful luxury brands of all time, synonymous with quality and craftsmanship. The company was founded in 1854 by Louis Vuitton, born on 4 August 1821, who at the age of 13 left his home in Anchay, eastern France, to walk to Paris, thus demonstrating his great determination at an early age. Once there, he became an apprentice to Monsieur Romain Maréchal – a well-respected box-maker and packer with a successful business in the famed Rue Saint-Honoré. Vuitton became a skilled craftsman who was totally devoted to his trade, but it was his innovative vision and creative flair that made fashion history.

On the following pages you will read about Vuitton's most ingenious creations, from the original Steamer trunk, designed with a flat top for easy stacking, to the Bed trunk that explorers would take on their missions. The numerous collaborations that have taken place over the years between the house of Louis Vuitton and many artists and brands created a dialogue between fashion and art – a concept spearheaded by Marc Jacobs, who became the company's Artistic Director in 1997. The huge celebrity following Louis Vuitton has enjoyed over the decades, from its early royal commissions, right up to Pharrell Williams's debut blockbuster celebrity menswear show in 2023, is also amply detailed. Finally, we go behind the scenes to look at how these masterpieces are created and how to authenticate a genuine piece, should you be searching for your quintessential Louis Vuitton travel companion on the preloved market.

Previous page: Actress Alicia Vikander fronts Louis Vuitton's 'Spirit of Travel', Autumn/Winter 2015 campaign, photographed by Patrick Demarchelier in Rio de Janeiro, Brazil.

Opposite: Travelling in style in head-to-toe Louis Vuitton, as seen in Dusseldorf, 2021.

CHAPTER

HOW IT ALL BEGAN

'Louis Vuitton is all about travel, that's the soul of the brand.'

Suzi Menkes, fashion journalist

LUXURY TRUNK-MAKING

The celebrated French fashion house Louis Vuitton Malletier, as it was first known, was founded in Paris in 1854. Synonymous with high-end fashion, today its offerings range from exquisite ready-to-wear collections to the finest of leather goods, shoes, perfumes, quality watches and jewellery, sunglasses and even books – primarily travel titles. Once a small family business that specialized in making premium luggage (*malletier* is French for 'trunk-maker'), today it is one of the world's most successful global luxury brands, still crafting exceptional equipment. And with over 460 stores in 50 different countries, it enjoys the status of being at the heart of the world's largest luxury goods conglomerate: Moët Hennessy Louis Vuitton (LVMH).

The history behind the French luxury fashion house begins with Monsieur Louis Vuitton, an outstanding master trunk-maker, who was born on 4 August 1821 in Anchay, a hamlet nestled in the mountainous Jura region in the east of France. He came from humble beginnings – a working-class family with a strong work ethic. His mother, a milliner, died when he was just ten years old, and his father, a farmer, passed away soon after he remarried. This prompted Louis to leave home when he was just 13, determined to make his way to Paris. He walked across the region, picking up work along the way until he reached his destination. Arriving at the capital in 1837, at the age of 16, he became an apprentice in a packing and box-making workshop. This was a highly respected profession at the time, as horse-drawn carriages were the primary mode of transport and wealthy travellers relied on such craftsmen (the *emballeur* and

Opposite: A stunning Louis Vuitton window display featuring a zebra in London's Bond Street store in 2011.

the *layetier*) to pack their precious belongings and protect them from being manhandled. He worked under the tutelage of Monsieur Romain Maréchal, whose successful studio was in the prestigious Rue Saint-Honoré. There, he learned the valuable art of making trunks, staying for 17 years, until he launched his own business. Under M. Maréchal he catered for the French court and aristocracy, who travelled regularly, and in 1853 was appointed personal trunk-maker and packer to the young Empress of the French, Eugénie de Montijo. Married to Emperor Napoleon III, the nephew of Napoleon Bonaparte, she was renowned for her love of fashion. Vuitton was in charge of transporting her luggage between Imperial residences, including the Tuileries Palace and her Biarritz villa, and such was his skill and uncompromising work ethic that he soon became known to the French elite, some of whom would become his future clients.

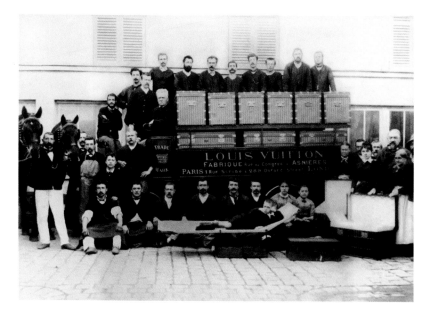

F. Fleury, Imprimeur-Éditeur, Paris

On 22 April 1854, Louis Vuitton married 17-year-old Clemence-Emilie Parriaux, and opened his first Parisian store at 4 Rue Neuve des Capucines, near the Place Vendôme, complete with a workshop. Outside, a sign read: 'Securely packs the most fragile objects. Specializing in packing fashions.' It was the beginning of the art of travel.

Above: *A signed postcard, circa 1905, depicting a traveller with his Louis Vuitton trunk.*

Opposite: *A family affair: Louis Vuitton sits in the driver's seat of his wagon with his employees in 1988. His son Georges appears next to him and his grandson Gaston-Louis Vuitton is in the bed trunk.*

THE CREATION OF MODERN LUGGAGE

During the nineteenth century, trunks were designed to be transported by carriages. They were rounded on the top, not only to let the user know where to open them, but also to allow the rain to run easily off their lids. They were made from animal skin (such as pigskin) and later from other leathers, so they were not entirely waterproof. But Vuitton's dedication and constant quest for innovation led him to experiment with different materials, such as specially treated lightweight canvas that was damage-resistant, which he used on a trunk commissioned by Empress Eugénie in 1865. The stylish masterpiece had a rounded lid and was light grey, a colour that became known as Trianon grey (used 1858–76). It matched the Empress's salons, and was considered very modern and chic, in contrast to most other trunks of the time, which were black or brown. This new, functional aesthetic revolutionized luggage, as the canvas was treated with glue and was therefore water-resistant, airtight, odourless and damp-proof. Vuitton also favoured lightweight poplar wood for the frames, and reinforced the luggage with more decorative beechwood. The Parisian aristocracy took note and soon Vuitton was very much in demand, coinciding with the dawn of transcontinental travel.

Louis Vuitton's vision and indisputable mastery of making luggage and travel accessories enabled him to create the state-of-the-art, sturdy and functional pieces the world required as it entered a new industrial age. Leisure travel, previously enjoyed exclusively by only a

Opposite: *The cover of the 1901 Louis Vuitton catalogue.*

very small elite, was now accessible to a wider audience, and soon trains, boats and automobiles – even aviation – were becoming increasingly popular. Luggage was now the new must-have and a status symbol for wealthy travellers worldwide.

Vuitton's first Steamer trunk, designed in 1858, was flat (not rounded) and easily stackable – a ground-breaking concept at the time. Such was its success, in fact, that the following year the business had to expand its workshop. Vuitton decided to relocate, and opened a new atelier in 18 Rue de Congrès, Asnières, north-east of Paris. Despite the demand, it was run as a workshop (not a production line) with 20 craftspeople working under the watchful eye of M. Vuitton, at benches in a flood-lit room with floor-to-ceiling windows made of glass and steel. The building also had two upper galleries where goods were displayed and sold to the public, and an apartment above it, where Louis Vuitton first lived with his family. During the 1900s the workforce grew to 100 and by 1914 Vuitton had recruited 225 artisans. Asnières became the centre of the House of Louis Vuitton and even today remains a symbol of its heritage. It is also where, in 1880, the designer built his family home. Today the historic Art Nouveau building is a private museum, complete with a renovated gallery space and a working atelier. There, 170 traditional trunk-makers continue to pass down their exceptional professional ability, as they create some of Vuitton's classic pieces as well as fulfil bespoke custom orders for discerning travellers.

Louis Vuitton's popularity continued to grow, and in 1867 he was awarded a bronze medal for his designs at the Exposition Universelle in Paris. Fame and status followed, and by 1869 he was supplying luggage to a number of heads of state, including Isma'il Pasha, the Khedive of Egypt. But things came to an abrupt halt during the Franco-Prussian War (1870–71), when his workshop

Above: An early Louis Vuitton label indicating their workshop and store addresses, as well as a serial number to identify its legitimacy.

was destroyed and looted. After the conflict, again with great determination, he rebuilt his Asnières atelier and opened new premises, this time at 1 Rue Scribe, Opéra. The new shop was strategically close to Paris's railway stations and to Le Grand Hôtel, the largest and most luxurious in Europe at the time – a smart and strategic move that ensured the constant flow of a wealthy clientele. It remained the Maison's flagship store until 1914.

Innovation continued, and a new Rayée canvas was introduced in 1872 – a striped design in red and beige – followed, in 1876, by a tan and beige version. It was a period known as the Deauville era, named after the fashionable seaside resort favoured by Parisian high society during the Belle Époque. The striped canvas (1872–88) became hugely popular, and firmly returned the luxury brand to its former pre-war glory. The following year, Georges Vuitton (1857–1936), Louis Vuitton's only son, returned, after studying in England for two years. Aged 16, he joined the Asnières workshop as an apprentice, where he was addressed as Monsieur Georges, and in time managed the Parisian store, freeing his father up to concentrate on creating new designs.

Above: *Rayée canvas was introduced in 1872 and became very popular among travellers during the Belle Époque.*

The brand's success was so unparalleled that it resulted in constant counterfeits. In an attempt to prevent further copies and to distinguish itself from cheaper replicas, in 1888 one of the brand's most iconic patterns was designed: the Damier. Still in use today, it is a chequerboard print in two-toned brown that had a logo inserted within the design, which read 'Marque L. Vuitton Déposée', ('L. Vuitton Registered Trademark'). A white and red version was also made, but was later discontinued. In 1998, the pattern was reintroduced and called the Damier Ebène. Variations of this canvas include the Damier Azur (2006) and the Damier Graphite (2008), released to mark its 120th anniversary.

Above: The chequerboard Damier pattern was created in 1888 to stand out from the competition.

Left: Custom designs, sometimes with initials or coloured stripes, were created for customers – as seen in this Damier trunk.

Keeping items safe at a time when travellers would transport many of their personal effects, including their precious valuables, was a constant challenge that troubled Louis Vuitton. He was a skilled locksmith and in 1886, after many years of extensive research and development, he arrived at a solution: an unpickable lock. The robust single lock system had two spring buckles and came with a single key, registered with a unique number, which would open every item in a customer's luggage collection. It was so successful that, in 1890, father and son patented the legendary mechanism, which is still in use today on all LV luggage. Furthermore, the Vuittons felt so confident that they publicly challenged the great American escape artist Harry Houdini to free himself from a locked LV trunk – an offer he allegedly ignored.

Such design milestones consolidated Louis Vuitton's outstanding craft and artistic flair. It reflected his ingenious mind, attention to detail, aesthetic sensitivity and complete devotion to his craft, which Louis enjoyed alongside his son, until he passed away on 27 February 1892, aged 72.

A further design intended to counter forgeries was created in 1896, with the company now under the premiership of Georges. A master of branding, he came up with one of the most identifiable and successful signature designs to date as a tribute to his late father. The canvas design, which has become known as the Monogram, alternated his father's initials with a quatrefoil shape and floral motif based on Japanese and Oriental imagery – a popular Victorian trend. This print, referred to as Meli-Melo in the variation for their baby range, was patented worldwide. Other more conservative canvas versions were also available at the time, in plain yellow, orange and brown.

Above: To protect the travellers' belongings, a single lock system was introduced in 1886. It had two spring buckles and a single key (top). In 1890 the Louis Vuitton lock was patented and is still in use today. Here is a version with the LV initials engraved on the metal (bottom).

THE NEXT GENERATIONS

After Louis Vuitton's death, the company was left solely to Georges, a true entrepreneur who shared his father's enthusiasm and love of innovation. He was instrumental in globalizing the brand and was keen to open it up to an international audience. Having already launched the first Louis Vuitton store outside France, in London's Oxford Street (1885), in 1893 he exhibited at the Chicago World's Fair. There, John Wanamaker, an American businessman who pioneered the notion of the department store, took an interest and established the brand in the USA. History was made once again in 1914, when Georges opened the world's largest luggage store on the Champs-Élysées, creating a stir among the Parisian fashion elite – including the celebrated Coco Chanel. More store openings followed, in cities including New York, Washington, Bombay and Buenos Aires.

Georges Vuitton, an excellent businessman, has been credited with elevating the reputation of his father's work and with creating the first luxury brand and lifestyle experience. During the famous great flood of the Seine in 1910, for instance, unable to fulfil his customers' orders, he saw a great opportunity: alongside his son Gaston-Louis, he created a number of exquisite small trunks with a zinc-planter interior, which they filled with flowers and delivered by boat to their most valued customers – by way of an apology. It was also later offered to pregnant customers. This successful tradition remains part of the history of the House of Luis Vuitton, with a reinterpretation of the original Flower trunk, the Malle Fleurs, still available today, measuring 29.5 (length) × 11.5 (height) × 14.5 cm (width) (11⅔ × 4½ × 5¾ in), with its water-resistant lining and metallic tray.

Opposite: The Louis Vuitton flagship store at Avenue des Champs-Élysées, opened in 1914.

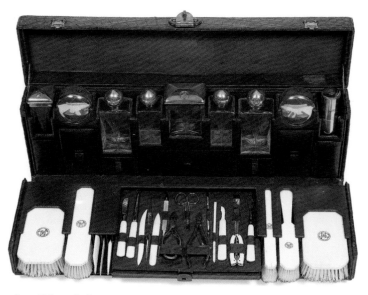

Above: *Beautifully crafted cases were made to include ivory brushes, glass bottles made by René Lalique and silverware by Jean Puiforcat.*

A love of automobiles was another of Georges Vuitton's defining traits and it inspired him to create a collection of trunks designed for long car journeys, offering travellers a way to transport their belongings – just as if they were taking a train. The first automobile trunk prototypes were presented at trade shows in 1897. Made to measure, they were sealed and covered in a sturdy canvas lining, called Vuittonite, made to match the car and designed to protect the contents from dust and rain. Georges created models for all eventualities, including lunch cases, tea cases, toiletry bags, pharmacy trunks and tool boxes. They could be placed in different parts of the car, with some fitting on a rack above the vehicle.

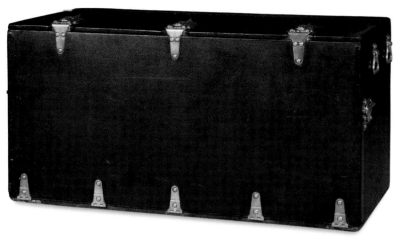

Above: A twentieth-century Louis Vuitton car trunk
in black Vuittonite canvas, circa 1910.

Below: Vuittonite canvas was used to create car trunks,
allowing drivers to transport their passengers' belongings
in style, as seen in this trunk, circa 1910.

Above: *This Louis Vuitton Malle Automobile Complète from 1916 was designed to be placed in the boot of the car for long journeys.*

Above: *The Louis Vuitton Malle Cabine trunk from 1921.*

The Maison's first travel bags were also designed during this time, such as the Steamer bag, created in 1901, originally called Inviolable, meaning 'unassailable'. Considered the perfect onboard companion for a cruise trip (and originally used as a laundry bag), it was also marketed for long car journeys and described in their catalogue as a 'convenient bag to carry rugs, pillows and travelling coats'. It had the advantage of folding flat so that it could be stored easily after use, using minimum space.

Following his spirit of adventure and adapting to new, exciting developments in aviation, in 1906 Georges set himself a new challenge: the creation of an unsinkable, watertight trunk. The Aero trunk was designed to accompany a helicopter prototype developed by his twin sons Jean and Pierre (who would sadly die in 1910 and 1917 respectively). It could also be fastened to the gondola of a hot air balloon and would stay afloat should it fall into the water. By 1927, the lightweight Aero had been adapted to commercial air travel, becoming their most popular style of trunk.

Georges Vuitton remained the head of the company until his death on 26 October 1936, aged 79. He was succeeded by Gaston-Louis Vuitton, his eldest son, who continued to take the Louis Vuitton empire into new, uncharted territory: the new era of aviation. A jovial character – 'I almost was born in a trunk!', he once said – he became known as 'the collector of objects' (he even loved to collect hotel labels), which reflected his fascination with, and love of, beautiful and delicate artifacts. Under his management, the company's portfolio was broadened to incorporate his interests, and in 1914 Louis Vuitton became a 'manufacturer of trunks, leather goods, goldsmith products and travel items'. More travel bags followed. A request from Coco Chanel in 1925 resulted in a domed bag called Squire, later renamed Alma, which led to holdalls such as

Above: *A Louis Vuitton Steamer trunk from the 1920s on display during the exhibition 'Dress Code: Are You Playing Fashion?' in 2021, shown at Bundeskunsthalle in Bonn, Germany.*

the Keepall and the smaller Speedy, initially called the Express (both of which were foldable and introduced in 1930). Their versatility struck a chord with a new, modern customer, who began using them for everyday personal use, as well as for travel. With functionality at heart, the Noé (originally designed to carry five champagne bottles) followed in 1932, as did the cylindrical-shaped Papillon, in 1966.

A self-made tycoon, Henri Racamier, who was married to Odile Vuitton, one of Louis Vuitton's great-granddaughters, inherited the business in 1977 and placed the focus on international expansion. Within ten years at the helm he had opened 100 stores worldwide, and in 1984, following his Financial Director Joseph Lafont's recommendation that the company should go public, the business ceased to be family-owned. Three years later, Louis Vuitton merged with luxury champagne brand Moët et Chandon and with spirits company Hennessy, forming the legendary and hugely successful conglomerate LVMH, which today owns over 75 luxury Maisons across the five major market sectors. Despite the merger, Louis Vuitton remains loyal to its heritage, values and innovative spirit – ingeniously adapting to the ever-changing times without compromising on enterprise, style, quality and craftsmanship.

Left: *A monogrammed canvas Louis Vuitton vanity case, circa 1980, with a leather handle, brass hardware and a single lock.*

Opposite: *A Noé bag, as seen on the catwalk during Paris Fashion Week for Autumn/Winter 2022.*

CHAPTER
2

LUGGAGE STYLES

'No dream is too large or object too complex.'

Louis Vuitton

VESSELS OF DREAMS

Described as vessels of dreams and treasure troves of stories, Louis Vuitton's many trunk designs tell the tale of the evolution of travel. With innovation and tradition at the heart of his trade, Monsieur Vuitton went on to create extraordinary pieces that adapted to the times – as journeys became more frequent, faster and eventually transcontinental. Several hundred variations were designed during his time – from bed trunks for military officers to hat boxes for transporting silk top hats. More recent ingenious additions to the Maison's legacy include the Malle Trainers in 2019 (in LV Monogram Eclipse, with 14 see-through monogrammed Perspex compartments for sneakers), Malle Maison Vivienne in 2020 (a pretty doll's house) and the Louis Vuitton Party trunk in 2021 (complete with a home bar, space for 30 bottles and a monogrammed disco ball).

The nineteenth century was the golden age of luggage, as travel became part of everyday life. Carriages were replaced by trains, boats and automobiles (and later aircraft), and storage space became limited. Adapting to modernity, trunks needed to be stacked, so Louis Vuitton began to build them with a flat lid. This made way for a whole array of styles, with very specific functions. There were also practical challenges to overcome: unlike a storage chest, the main function of a trunk was to transport goods, and while needing to remain strong, it also had to be as light as possible. This is why Vuitton combined light poplar wood, beech and gaboon viper skin to increase shock absorption, and reinforced the surfaces and corners of his creations. At first, he used wooden slats, metal, brass, leather and sometimes cardboard, and later preferred lozine, a chemically treated, wood-based compound that was light but durable.

Opposite: *Sean Connery photographed by Annie Leibowitz near his Bahamas residence for the Louis Vuitton Core Values campaign (2007–12).*

THE STEAMER

Possibly the most iconic trunk to date, this is also the most sought-after in the preloved market, because it can be used in so many ways. Regarded as an *objet d'art*, it comes in many different sizes, and is often used as a storage chest – or even a coffee table, by simply placing a sheet of glass on the top. Nicky Hilton Rothschild uses one as a side table in her New York City penthouse; designer Sig Bergamin has two, stacked at the end of his bed, to be used as ottomans, in his home in São Paulo; and Michael Kors has one in his wardrobe.

Steamer trunks, known as Malles Courrier (mail trunks in English), were widely used when train travel and boats became a standardized mode of transport. Their name derives from the fact that they would leave at the same time as the mail, whether on a steam train or on an ocean liner. Louis Vuitton had introduced his first series of flat trunks, covered in Trianon grey canvas, which were rectangular in shape, in 1858. Other canvas designs followed, as mentioned in the previous chapter, from striped (Rayée) to a checked pattern (Damier), as well as other plain colours. Later, in 1896, the legendary Louis Vuitton Monogram print was designed by Georges Vuitton in memory of his father.

Adjusting to the changing concept of travelling, the Steamer fell into two categories: men's and women's trunks, the latter being taller to accommodate the fashions of the time. Typically, a man's trunk measured 45–55 cm (17¾–21⅔ in) in length, while a woman's was 80–110 cm (31½–43⅓ in), with some of the oldest catalogues showing models with a length of up to 130 cm (51⅕ in). Inside, they were entirely lined and would often have a grid pattern on the lid, made of a lattice of ribbon, for placing cards and other documents. They would also have movable trays that acted as compartments,

Above: *The Steamer trunk was made with canvas, as seen in this example from 1910.*
.

usually arranged in three tiers. On the outside, most of these early trunks had a leather strap, as well as wooden laths used as reinforcement, and they would be secured with brass clasps and a lock. The handles, in brass or leather, were there to allow the trunk to be moved sideways, by a concierge for instance. In order to identify its legitimacy, the hardware had a serial number and the Louis Vuitton address stamped on it, as well as a label on the inside of the trunk.

Most Wanted: Louis Vuitton x Supreme Malle Courrier 90

This true collector's item was designed in 2017 by the then Creative Director of Louis Vuitton, British designer Kim Jones. As part of a collaboration with the American clothing and skateboarding lifestyle brand Supreme, it significantly elevated streetwear into the luxury arena. Inside, the trunk was lined and included organizer trays. On the outside, natural leather handles, lozine slats and golden brass locks completed the design. The Malle Courrier 90 trunk featured an LV Monogram in Supreme's signature red which, as Kim Jones said, gave it 'that kind of Pop Art feeling'.

The trunk retailed at $68,500, reaching $150,000 in the preloved market, and measured 56.5 × 75.6 × 48.9 cm (22¼ × 29¾ × 19¼ in). As part of this collaboration, a matching skateboard carrier trunk (supplied with a skateboard, wheels, a tool kit, shoulder straps and a linen bag) was also issued for international skatepark lovers, priced at $54,500.

Above: A red Louis Vuitton x Supreme trunk is displayed during a preview at Sotheby's for their inaugural hip-hop auction in New York City, in September 2020.

THE WARDROBE TRUNK

The Malle Armoire, or Wardrobe trunk, is a vertical piece of luggage that has two fitted-out halves. It should not be mistaken for the Cabin trunk, which was lower, at around 30 cm (12 in) in height, and could be stored under the bed in the cabin of a steam liner.

Above: Michelle Williams fronting a Louis Vuitton campaign in 2013, with a timeless Wardrobe trunk in the background.

Left: *This fabulous Louis Vuitton trunk accommodates 30 pairs of shoes and was named after the French actress and opera singer Lili Pons, who requested a shoe trunk to take with her when on tour.*

Although the portable armoire was introduced in 1875, it wasn't until the 1890s that it became a true symbol of Parisian elegance, accommodating the changing, more fluid fashion silhouettes. Some of the early models had a rounded top to ensure that they were placed the right way up, and they would often have wooden feet on the base. Side handles would also be provided to help tilt the piece onto a trolley or to be moved sideways – but not to carry it, as the trunks alone weighed around 45–50 kg (100–110 lb) when empty.

Given that, at the time, fashionable travellers would change outfits several times a day, the main advantage these trunks offered was, of course, that they didn't have to be unpacked, thanks to the different storage solutions they provided inside. The most common model, when upright, opened by lifting the top section first, and had a wardrobe space on one side with hangers (called 'princess hangers') and drawers on the other, although sometimes they were configured as either just hanging space or just drawers. They could also be customized and adapted to special requests, so they might have an iron and ironing board, or perhaps secret drawers concealed behind existing ones. Keeping up with the latest fashions and travel needs, the Wardrobe trunk was constantly being reinvented. In 1905, a model called the Ideal trunk, Malle Idéale, was designed to fit a gentleman's essential wardrobe. Fit for a dandy, it had the dimensions of a large Steamer trunk but opened in two sections from the middle outwards and came with precise instructions as to what to pack where. It was made either in leather or covered in Louis Vuitton's Monogram canvas.

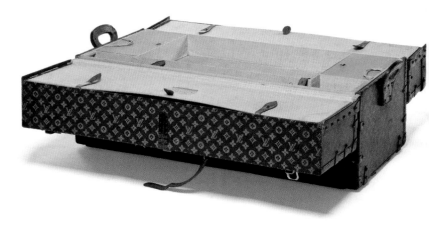

Above: Louis Vuitton trunks had many compartments to fit their customers' needs, and some even had secret drawers. This is the Ideal trunk., which opened in two sections.

The standard sizes and distributions for a wardrobe trunk (as stated in a 1914 Louis Vuitton catalogue) were as follows. For women, the trunk would measure 125 × 57 × 55 cm (49¼ × 22½ × 21⅔ in); the more expensive ones had a depth of 65 cm (25⅔ in) instead and would have a wardrobe on one side and drawers on the other. They were designed to fit up to 18 dresses and accessories such as shoes, hats and gloves. The men's equivalent measured 135 × 57 × 55 cm (53⅛ × 22½ × 21¾ in), with space for coats and hats. But sometimes, in order to meet the standards of American railway companies, they measured just 115 × 57 × 55 cm (45¼ × 22½ × 21⅔ in).

Variations on this trunk were the Malle Chemise, or Shirt trunk, which, when opened, revealed a chest of usually three drawers, and the Malle Commode trunk, or Trouser trunk, a similar piece of luggage designed to carry trousers.

Most Wanted: The Baby Wardrobe Trunk

This new addition to the Vuitton trunk family was introduced in 2023 as part of a capsule collection that included toys, clothing and accessories. The trunk measures 48.5 × 89.5 × 55 cm (19 × 35¼ × 21⅔ in), is equipped with two mirrors, three small hangers and has eight different-sized drawers to accommodate all of an infant's essentials. It has a lock closure with golden buckles and features the quintessential brown Monogram canvas. A Baby suitcase is also available. On the outside it has a cream jacquard Monogram pattern (made using organic cotton) with natural leather detailing (made from responsibly sourced Leather Working Group-certified materials), and a yellow stitched trim with matching interior. A treasured piece, no doubt to be handed down through generations.

THE TRUNK BED

The trunk Bed or camp-bed was created in the mid-1860s, primarily for use in military campaigns and trips overseas. A precursor to the concept of 'glamping', this travel companion was, put simply, a bed in a trunk. It was also used by explorers, who would take it on colonial expeditions. The lined mattress was placed on a base that had wooden upright ledges, resembling narrow headboards, often on either end, and legs that could be unfolded.

Most Wanted: Pierre Savorgnan de Brazza's Trunk

The best-known example of this style of trunk was that belonging to explorer Pierre Savorgnan de Brazza who, in 1875, in preparation for his first expeditions, ordered a set of Louis Vuitton luggage. It included a trunk Bed and some zinc and copper trunks, which would protect their contents from insects and moisture and be adaptable to the destination's climate. The lining inside the trunk Bed and the fabric

Right: An explorer's dream: the Louis Vuitton trunk Bed in Damier canvas, 1891.

of the mattress featured red and cream stripes, and the trunk itself measured 90 × 45 × 55 cm (35½ × 17¾ × 21⅔ in) when closed, 90 × 200 cm (35½ × 78¾ in) when fully opened, and weighed 65 kg (143 lb). In 1879, the explorer ordered a further trunk Bed with a secret drawer, which he used to hide sensitive information he collected for the French government. Some even say that Louis Vuitton himself was needed to reopen the concealed drawer.

A hard-wearing explorer collection was created by the Maison to accompany the trunk Bed, designed for adventurers of the time. Today, the pieces that were made of zinc, copper, aluminium and brass are hugely sought-after. An aluminium-bound trunk was sold in 2018 at auction for a record-breaking £162,500; and, in 2023, a rare zinc Malle Cabine trunk sold for £66,000.

THE DESK TRUNK

The Malle Bureau, or Desk trunk, became popular in the early twentieth century. With the intellectual traveller in mind, it was designed in many different configurations and finishes, some more or less complex, reflecting the customer's wishes. In 1904, exiled Russian Princess Lobanov de Rostov acquired a Malle Bureau, referred to as the Scented Desk trunk, which, they say, was lined in pink satin and perfumed with Guerlain's Heliotrope fragrance. It was one of the five trunks with which she and her 20 servants travelled. Another model, from 1916, opened horizontally: you lifted the top and there were two doors on the front-facing panel. Once opened, these created a frame that would secure a table top, below which was a section with drawers and stationery compartments. Also known as Secretary trunks, they were sometimes configured vertically, with the front panel acting as a single door. A small working desk that was made to fit a typewriter would fold out from the door while drawers in the trunk doubled up as an office space.

Most Wanted: The Stokowski Trunk

Perhaps the most notable example of a Louis Vuitton Malle Bureau was the one designed in the 1930s for the conductor Leopold Stokowski. Referred to as the Stokowski trunk, this ingenious piece of furniture was created as a portable office for the musician to take with him when on tour. Covered in Monogram canvas, it opened vertically. The top side would open like a lid and the front panel became a door that folded back on itself against the left wall of the trunk. In this position, the panel would reveal a drop-leaf table with legs. The central body of the trunk had two shelves and two drawers with pull-handles below them to store items such as stationery, music scores and notebooks.

Inspired by the Stokowski trunk, a state-of-the-art trunk – and a dream for modern musicians and high-flying DJs – was unveiled in 2018 in Shanghai. The DJ trunk, a collaboration between Louis Vuitton and the French audio technology company Devialet, was designed to fit Phantom speakers, a turntable, headphones, a mixer and a computer. The trunk is covered in Eclipse Monogram canvas (grey and black) with matching ruthenium hardware; inside, it is covered with grey microfibre, and the table is lined with premium black cowhide. A bag comes with this trunk, so you can carry your 20 favourite vinyl records.

Right: The Stokowski trunk was designed for the renowned orchestra director Leopold Stokowski. A portable office, it had shelves, drawers and a table for a typewriter.

LIBRARY TRUNKS

Books and travelling have always gone hand in hand, and the Library trunk was created for travellers with a love of literature. Before paperbacks were available, many trunks were designed specifically to transport heavy book collections on long journeys. One such trunk was created to carry the Encyclopaedia Britannica (circa 1911). This was a made-to-measure, long and narrow trunk in Monogram canvas with brass rivets, a leather top handle and two side latches. Other designs resembled a travel library, and were engineered like a Wardrobe trunk; instead of drawers or hanging space, they had shelving on either side. A further Library trunk design would be placed on its side when opened, enabling the lid to become the top shelf of the transportable bookcase. More variations included Bureau trunks, which combined bookshelves for the traveller's favourite literature, with drawers to organize their paperwork.

Most Wanted: The Hemingway Trunk

An exceptional Library trunk, with a very special story, was designed in 1927 by Gaston-Louis Vuitton, a self-confessed bibliophile: the trunk was custom-made and delivered to the American novelist Ernest Hemingway. Covered in Monogram canvas and with the usual lozine slats to protect its borders, the trunk had two brass clasps on either side that were signed and numbered, plus two more on the front and a leather handle attached to the top. Inside were seven drawers to accommodate books and documents, including a main drawer to fit a typewriter, as well as shelves and secret drawers. When opened, the mechanism held the trunk up, ensuring that it didn't collapse. For some time Hemingway's 'travel companion' was thought to be lost, but it was allegedly found in the basement of Ritz

Hotel in Paris in 1944, together with the manuscript of his long-lost posthumous masterpiece *A Moveable Feast.* This trunk became known as the Hemingway model.

above: The Hemingway trunk was brought to life by Gaston-Louis Vuitton and delivered to the author in May 1927. It had shelving and drawers – some secret and one to fit his typewriter.

THE STEAMER BAG

Throughout its history, one of the Maison's greatest strengths has been the ability to adapt to new emerging transport technologies, hand luggage being the perfect example. The first hand luggage created by Louis Vuitton was the Steamer bag in 1901; it was designed to be folded up into a Steamer trunk when empty. Also known as the Sac Weekend, it was originally used inside the trunk as a laundry bag, separating fresh clothes from those already worn on a long sea voyage (on a yacht or ocean liner), but it could also be taken on board as a small holdall. This was an inspired concept, which enabled passengers to carry some of their essential belongings with them. A striking personalized version was designed by Gaston-Louis Vuitton, featuring a black 'V' in the centre with blue, red and white (the colours of the French national flag) in the background – a logo that was relaunched during the Spring/Summer 2005 catwalk collection. Different iterations of the Steamer bag are available on the vintage market, and a number of updated versions of this classic are also available from Louis Vuitton boutiques and online.

Left: A Steamer bag on display at the Louis Vuitton Voyages exhibition in Beijing, to mark the French fashion house's twentieth year in China.

above: Designed in 1901 as the first piece of hand luggage, the canvas Monogram Steamer bag is the perfect companion for any traveller.

Most Wanted: The Steamer PM

Echoing the shape of its original predecessor, this versatile, wide-opening bag can be carried by hand using a single top handle, or worn crossbody with a removable, adjustable strap. It combines exotic black crocodile leather with the classic brown Monogram canvas, and is updated with dark hardware, including a chain-and-pin closure. It measures 38 × 39 × 15 cm (15 × 15⅓ × 6 in).

THE SPEEDY

Launched in 1930, the functional Speedy was originally crafted in plain leather. It came with a lock and was called the Express, reflecting the increasing pace of the times. The following year it was made in Monogram cotton canvas (using a single piece of fabric, so that the Monogram is inverted on one side), adding to its glamour status. It was made in three sizes: 30, 35 and 40 cm (12, 14 and 16 in). A new addition to the range, a smaller Speedy at 25 cm (10 in), became a staple after it was requested by Audrey Hepburn in 1965. She carried it everywhere (as did Jackie Kennedy and Lauren Bacall), because it was perfect for travelling; like the Steamer, it could be folded flat and packed into a suitcase. Such was Hepburn's love for this piece that she was even spotted carrying two of them during the 1980s. Considered one of Louis Vuitton's iconic classics, the Speedy has been at the centre of many collaborations between the Maison and a select number of cherry-picked artists. Some of the most noteworthy include Takashi Murakami's Speedy Multicolore (a multicoloured redesign of the classic Monogram, favoured by Paris Hilton and Nicole Ritchie), Stephen Sprouse's Graffiti (launched in 2001) and his rose designs (part of Sprouse's tribute collection in 2009), and both of Yayoi Kusama's artistic projects in 2012 and 2023. The latter were variations on her signature infinity dot designs.

Opposite: A brown Speedy Bandoulière 30, with its removable strap, is the perfect accessory to dress up any look – as worn in Berlin, 2020.

Most Wanted: Stephen Sprouse's Graffiti Speedy

This partnership marked a special moment in fashion history. With Sprouse 'defacing' the classic Monogram and updating it with a graffiti print, one could say that fashion and art amalgamated, breaking barriers and adding a new dimension to popular culture. As Yves Carcelle (Louis Vuitton's CEO, 1990–2012) said, 'For me, this Monogram Graffiti was the first milestone of our permanent reinvention of our history.'

The original Louis Vuitton Monogram Graffiti Speedy (2001), came in pale colours such as khaki and white. Later, in 2009, it was relaunched in bright orange, strong pink and neon green. The bag had gold hardware and a lock and key, with a brown canvas lining inside.

Above: *Electric blue and iridescent Speedy bags, in Paris in 2019.*

Opposite: *Stephen Sprouse's Graffiti collaboration, as seen on the catwalk for Spring/Summer 2001. Marc Jacobs called the bags 'anti-snob snobbism'.*

THE ALZER SUITCASE

Always ahead of its time, the House of Louis Vuitton first created cases for suits – or suitcases – circa 1875, when they designed the Porte-habits Rigide and later the Porte-habits à Soufflet in 1892. Both were based on the shape of the Malle Armoire, the predecessor of all Louis Vuitton suitcases, and looked like small, slight trunks with a handle. Then, during the 1950s, as travellers took to the skies in large numbers and air voyages became shorter and more frequent, hand luggage became *de rigueur.* As a response, Vuitton designed the slimmer and lighter Alzer suitcase, which is still in production today. This luxurious item soon became indispensable to a new generation of seasoned passengers, who would carry it from terminal to aircraft and back again, and place it either in the hold or in an overhead compartment.

The Alzer comes in several sizes: 60, 65, 70, 75 and 80 cm (23⅔, 25⅔, 27½, 29½ and 31½ in wide). It is mostly seen in Monogram canvas. If you're vintage shopping, however, you may come across versions in plain soft leather (for example, in brown, black and red) and Damier canvas – including the Azur check. The hardware is mostly brass (two spring latches and corner protectors), and it comes with a key to open the ingenious unpickable lock. The inside is lined, and has a tray insert that can be taken out. The Alzer also comes with a removable protective storage cover.

Many other styles followed, including the Porte-documents Voyage, which came out in 1981, and the smaller Valise Cotteville, which launched in 1999. These were either covered in leather, canvas, Vuittonite or exotic skins, and inside they had straps to secure clothing and other items.

Opposite: Eva Herzigová featuring in the Louis Vuitton Autumn/Winter campaign 2002, photographed by Mert and Marcus.

Above: *Spacious, light and incomparably sturdy, with a convenient removable tray, the Alzer has a central S lock reinforced by two side latches.*

Left: *The Epi black leather was used for several classic Louis Vuitton products, including the Alzer suitcase and the Alma bag seen here.*

Most Wanted: Black Leather Alzer

Over time, the Alzer suitcase has been released in different finishes, including a striking black Epi leather version, where the skin is tanned and pressed to create a textured finish. These are currently only available on the preloved market and come in a variety of sizes. They have a matching black handle and contrasting gold hardware. Lined in grey suede, inside they have two cream canvas straps and a removable tray.

SPECIAL COMMISSIONS

The House of Louis Vuitton has created countless custom orders over the years – some eccentric, some fascinating – specifically designed for its most valued and imaginative clients. The very first commission was a special photographer's trunk built for French banker and philanthropist Albert Kahn, well-known for collecting photographic material. Produced in 1929, this trunk was red and displayed in the right-hand corner the three white 'X's that resembled birds in mid-flight, which were Khan's trademark signature. The trunk had contrasting black hardware, and the interior was lined with linen. Another special trunk was made in 1924 for René Gimpel, a French art dealer who used it to carry precious works of art around the world. This idea was repeated in 2018 when Louis Vuitton designed a trunk to transport Johannes Vermeer's *The Milkmaid* from Amsterdam's Rijksmuseum to the

Above: *A 1926 Tea Case made of Épi leather, custom-made for the Maharaja of Baroda.*

Ueno Royal Museum in Tokyo. It had a yellow interior to match the milkmaid's bodice. There was also a Tea Case made for the Maharaja of Baroda in 1926 and a very special royal commission in 1936, made for France and Marianne, the dolls belonging to the future Queen Elizabeth II and her sister Margaret. The beautiful trunks were, of course, tiny, but exquisite and perfectly formed.

The number of bespoke orders for jet-setters is endless, and include a trunk designed to fit exactly 1,000 Havana cigars (with a built-in barometer to regulate humidity), one to accommodate a set of Christmas tree decorations, another to keep a croquet set, and one to carry a rubber duck that stayed in the Louis Vuitton workshop long enough to be nicknamed 'Louis'.

Above: An early twentieth-century Monogram trunk, custom-built to fit 60 watches.

Above: *The ultimate luxury: a portable cocktail bar with a humidor for 300 cigars. Using the finest Spanish cedar wood, the shelves are removable and adjustable.*

Most Wanted: The Petite Malle

When Nicolas Ghesquière took over as Creative Director at Louis Vuitton in 2013, one of the first things he designed was a Petite Malle, or Small trunk, presented in his first show (Autumn/Winter 2014) as a handbag. It is based on Vuitton's first custom trunk created for M. Kahn and, in a nod to the brand's heritage and rich history, it features the iconic three 'X's in the right-hand corner. This modern classic, available in-store, online and on the second-hand market, is constantly reinvented. From a hot pink Monogram pattern carefully embroidered into the leather to a version with multicoloured strips of canvas (like those found on Parisian café chairs), or a red one emulating the original customized luxury trunk (featuring the three 'X' design in the corner, see below), it is a little piece of Vuitton history that encapsulates the brand's vision, functionality and effortless style. The Petite Malle measures 20 × 12.5 × 6 cm (8 × 5 × 2⅓ in).

Above: The Louis Vuitton Petite Malle Damier clutch, designed for Autumn/Winter 2014.

CHAPTER

SPECIAL EDITIONS

'I think what we are doing at Vuitton, in bringing other people in to re-look and re-see something as iconic as the Monogram, I think it just makes perfect sense.'

Marc Jacobs,
fashion designer and Artistic Director
of Louis Vuitton, 1997–2014

KEY COLLABORATIONS

A new chapter in the Louis Vuitton story began in 1997, when Marc Jacobs was appointed Artistic Director for the House to create their first ready-to-wear clothing line. This bold move elevated the brand from luxury travel to high fashion, and Jacobs's inspired and fresh approach enabled him to stay true to its core values. He also started a new trend and paved the way for future fashion houses when he invited designers, architects and artists to collaborate with the Maison. 'What I have in mind are things that are deluxe but that you can also throw into a bag and escape town with, because Louis Vuitton has a heritage in travel,' he told American *Vogue*. A new following was created with the birth of these limited-edition collaborations, which are sometimes seen as an investment, as the items can often reach a much higher price when resold on the preloved market.

Opposite: Louis Vuitton's collaboration with Yayoi Kusama in 2012 included some pumpkin dots, as seen in this Keepall Bandoulière.

STEPHEN SPROUSE

Louis Vuitton's Spring/Summer 2001 show opened with a bang when five male models walked down the catwalk each holding trunks and several pieces of luggage, all of which were covered in coloured graffiti that read 'LOUIS VUITTON PARIS'. Jacobs had invited the influential New York artist and fashion designer Stephen Sprouse to work on a line of accessories for Louis Vuitton, creating this fun and vibrant – if slightly subversive – limited-edition collection. It was a pivotal moment in fashion history that blurred the boundaries between fashion and art: a concept to which the artist, the first of many collaborators, firmly subscribed. Jacobs repositioned the legendary luggage brand by reworking the classic Monogram canvas that was the very essence of the history of Louis Vuitton – like a coat of arms or family crest. Sprouse 'defaced' the Monogram with great dynamism by superimposing freehand graffiti over it – in muted colours such as white and green – on both luggage and accessories, creating 'a new surface and a new meaning with something old', as Marc Jacobs explained. It was a tremendous achievement, a *chef-d'oeuvre*; and, in 2009, the Sprouse × Louis Vuitton collaboration was relaunched, this time solely under Marc Jacobs, as Sprouse had died of cancer in 2004. 'I did my best in a first-degree way, to imitate what I think Stephen would have done, or has done in terms of fashion,' said Jacobs. The tribute revival was released with Monogram Graffiti pieces in bright pink, orange and green, and some rose prints over the LV Monogram, which Sprouse had designed in 2001.

Opposite: *Agyness Deyn attends a tribute to Stephen Sprouse hosted by Louis Vuitton, at the Bowery Ballroom in New York in 2009.*

Overleaf: *A display showing the collection of Stephen Sprouse's Graffiti bags in different colourways.*

RICHARD PRINCE

Another iconic collaboration took place in 2008 between the House and the American artist Richard Prince, known widely for his pioneering of 'appropriation art', and for his abstract, brightly coloured paintings. Marc Jacobs, a fan and collector of his art, invited him to work on his interpretation of the classic Monogram. This resulted in several variants, most notably his Aquarelle print (a 'smudged' watercolour version of the Monogram in 17 delicate colours, ranging from pink and purple to orange and yellow and printed on a white and brown background), seen on bags and luggage, such as the Weekender and the Speedy.

He also worked on an abstract series for which he fused different techniques that treated the canvas to look like it was worn out or distressed. Some pieces displayed coated denim washes, while others were spray-painted or had splattered colours and jokes printed on them. This collaboration made the fashion headlines in 2008 when it featured in the *Sex and the City* movie: one of the bags (the Motard Firebird) was given by Carrie Bradshaw (played by Sarah Jessica Parker) to her assistant Louise (played by Jennifer Hudson), so that she too could have her very own Vuitton to cherish.

Above: The Richard Prince x Louis Vuitton collaboration was very experimental. The Jaune Denim Defile Weekender PM Pulp bag is made from stonewashed Monogram denim canvas and coated with PVC.

Overleaf: A line of models hold Richard Prince x Louis Vuitton bags at the opening of Richard Prince's exhibition in 2007, at the Guggenheim Museum in New York City.

TAKASHI MURAKAMI

Described by British *Vogue* as the defining fashion collaboration of the noughties, and by *Time* magazine as the 'number one' moment in fashion of 2003, the blockbuster collaboration between Vuitton and Murakami was to become a huge success that has stood the test of time.

Japanese contemporary artist Takashi Murakami, acclaimed for his Superflat two-dimensional work, and who enjoys blurring the line between high and low culture through his pop art aesthetic, redesigned the classic Monogram playfully. He produced a pattern in 33 carefully selected colours, the Monogram Multicolore, on both white and black backgrounds. Murakami wasn't aware of the Louis Vuitton brand prior to their approaching him, and his brief from Jacobs gave him total freedom: 'I don't know. It doesn't matter. Do whatever you like,' he replied when the artist asked him for guidelines. First revealed at the Spring/Summer 2003 Louis Vuitton show, the print was soon seen everywhere, on different bag styles – the Speedy, the Alma and the Papillon – and it was on everyone's arm. It was loved by celebrities when it was launched (Paris Hilton, Lindsay Lohan and Jessica Simpson to name a few) and has recently enjoyed a comeback in the vintage market, as it was discontinued in 2015 (as seen carried by Kendall Jenner and Bella Hadid).

As well as bags and hand luggage, the print also covered a Steamer trunk, which was presented in 2007. Dubbed the Marilyn, this limited-edition piece was part of a retrospective exhibition at the Museum of Contemporary Art in Los Angeles, and a fine example of the growing merging relationship between fashion and

Opposite: Austin entertainer Lamar Sanchez with a Louis Vuitton black Monogram Multicolore Boite Flacons vanity case at 'The Crown We Never Take Off' Art Basel Exhibit in Miami in 2022.

art. 'Just like contemporary art, fashion is about history,' said Murakami in an interview with Mariko Tishitani. It sold for $500,000 and was designed to display 33 LV × Murakami bags, carefully positioned at an angle. The trunk had some drawers, and its exterior was made of multicoloured Monogram canvas, natural cowhide leather, brass and wood. The bags were made of the same multicolour canvas, alligator leather and brass. The piece measured 99.6 × 57.1 × 64.7 cm (39¼ × 22½ × 25½ in) when closed.

Opposite: *A pink poodle with a Louis Vuitton suitcase and a carrying case for her pet human. Illustration by Ana Lense-Larrauri, 2003.*

Overleaf left: *Louis Vuitton's Spring/Summer 2003 collection featured the Takashi Murakami x Louis Vuitton collaboration.*

Overleaf right: *Eva Herzigová is photographed by Mert and Marcus for Louis Vuitton's Spring/Summer 2003 campaign, featuring Murakami's Cherry Blossom collection.*

YAYOI KUSAMA

Yayoi Kusama is considered one of the most influential artists of our time. When Marc Jacobs first asked to visit her at her Shinjuku studio in Japan, she, like Murakami, had no idea who or what Louis Vuitton was. Some time later, Louis Vuitton offered to support a solo exhibition she held at the Tate Modern in London, which led to their first collaboration together in 2012. In preparation for this, Kusama received a sample of the 1896 Monogram, and was asked to reinterpret it. After some brainstorming, their first joint venture came to life, based on the signature polka dot art she has developed since the 1970s. Her delicate, repetitive and almost hypnotic design was based on infinity and expansion, a lifelong theme in her artistic journey, inspired by the hallucinations she experienced at the age of ten, which she described as 'flashes of light, auras, or dense fields of dots'. Creating beauty through art and communicating her thoughts to the world became her therapy. As the Louis Vuitton press release explains, 'Yayoi Kusama's collaboration in 2012 flourished through various universes of the Maison, from exhibitions, products and a series of unique window installations, which included a startingly life-like mannequin modelled after the artist herself.' Kusama's polka dot patterns, op-art pumpkins and tendril patterns were found on many items – classic totes, suitcases, watches and shoes. A trunk was also made, which she hand-painted using acrylic paint, again with her signature infinity dots.

Opposite: Model Gisele Bündchen fronted the 2023 campaign for Louis Vuitton x Yayoi Kusama.

New, original and colourful motifs were introduced for a second collaboration in 2023, including figurative flowers, pumpkins, 'faces' and her iconic infinity dots imagined by the artist, who was 94 at the time. A global campaign launched the collection, some of its highlights being a robot of the artist featured in a New York Vuitton store, an inflatable Kusama floating 30 m (100 ft) above the Paris boutique and an effigy of herself displayed in the prestigious Harrods store in London. The print was featured across ready-to-wear, selected leather goods, bags (including the Speedy and the Alma), suitcases, trunks and shoes. A combination of old craftmanship and new techniques was employed, such as multistep serigraphy, which replicated her vibrant brushstrokes by adding volume to the print, making it look as if it had just been hand-painted. Some of the pieces also included metal studs inspired by the artist's 1966 Venice Biennale installation, *Narcissus Garden*, with mirrors that looked like mercury droplets, which added a sculptural dimension to the design.

Above: Louis Vuitton's collaboration with Yayoi Kusama in 2012 included pumpkin dots, as seen in this Keepall Bandoulière.

Opposite: A sculpture of Yayoi Kusama on the Avenue des Champs-Élysées, 2023.

OBJETS NOMADES

To celebrate Louis Vuitton's spirit of travel, in 2012 the Maison invited a number of designers to create functional furniture and travel accessories. These limited-edition pieces include hammocks and foldable stools, and they combine exceptional craftsmanship, creativity and innovation. India Mahdavi, Marcel Wanders, Patricia Urquiola, Fernando and Humberto Campana and Atelier Oï were some of the designers enlisted. Some of these creations were showcased in the 2016 Louis Vuitton exhibition 'Volez, Voguez, Voyagez' at the Grand Palais in Paris and in Kioicho, Tokyo. This is an ongoing initiative that can be accessed online (amazingly, with the aid of Augmented Reality technology, you can even visualize some of the Objets Nomades in your own home) and in-store.

Above and opposite: *Louis Vuitton commissioned Andrew Kudless to design furniture for the Objets Nomades limited-edition collection, presented at Design Miami in 2019 (above). The Louis Vuitton exhibition at Design Miami in 2021 (opposite).*

THE CHAPMAN BROTHERS

The provocative British design duo Jake and Dinos Chapman, known for their controversial approach to art, collaborated with Louis Vuitton on two occasions. The first was in 2013, when Kim Jones (then Artistic Director of the menswear collections), commissioned them to design a print for the label's Autumn/Winter collection. It was a surreal flora and fauna pattern called Garden in Hell, which incorporated intertwined flowers, eyeballs and fantastical-looking creatures (some of them screaming) on either a red or a navy background.

Another collaboration with the Chapman Brothers, in 2017, featured a design that was equally fascinating – if a touch sinister. Inspired by Kim Jones, who lived in Africa as a child, it featured wild animals, including lions, elephants, giraffes and zebras, on a Monogram Savane canvas in Ink and Dune shades. The collection, for Spring/Summer 2017, covered small leather goods, clothing, accessories and luggage. The animals looked like distorted sketches, as if seen through warped glass, and had large, piercing eyes and fierce, aggressive facial expressions that added to the overall punk aesthetic of the collection. In his show notes, Jones explained: 'There's always something a little London hidden somewhere, though. This time, it is the influence of punk – albeit via Africa ….' From luggage tags to trunks, the illustrations were featured on the Monogram (Monogram Savane), and on the classic Damier (Damier Savane) prints. There were also fun clear Perspex trunks, which seemed to contain the raging animals, and had rings on the side that could transform them into backpacks.

Opposite: The Chapman Brothers created the 'Garden in Hell' prints that featured on jackets, dressing gowns and accessories at the Louis Vuitton Autmn/Winter menswear show, 2013.

Overleaf: A blue Monogram Chapman Brothers' Keepall and Savana PM bag featuring a lion.

JEFF KOONS

The LV × Koons Masters (1 and 2 collections, April and October 2017, respectively), was a collaboration with American neo-pop artist Jeff Koons, known for his conceptual artwork and kitsch aesthetic (his work includes sculptures such as oversized stainless-steel balloon animals). Koons reproduced a selection of classic masterpieces for this venture, such as Leonardo da Vinci's *Mona Lisa* (circa 1503) and Monet's *Water Lilies* (1916). The images were printed onto canvas using the latest technology. Koons added the artist's name on the front of the items and his own initials in a corner, adopting the font of the classic Louis Vuitton monogrammed initials. It was featured on a number of bags and accessories, including a backpack, the Speedy, the Keepall and the Neverfull.

Left: The Masters collaboration between Louis Vuitton and Jeff Koons featured Leonardo da Vinci's Mona Lisa, seen here in a window display in 2017, in the New Bond Street boutique in London.

Opposite: A limited-edition bag in Monogram Eclipse from the Fragment Design x Louis Vuitton collection, spotted on the streets of Paris.

FRAGMENT DESIGN

Known as the godfather of streetwear, Hiroshi Fujiwara, founder of Fragment Design, collaborated with Louis Vuitton under Kim Jones for their Autumn/Winter 2017 pre-collection, which launched in Tokyo. The capsule collection was inspired by the 1980s fashion aesthetic – the New York downtown art and hip-hop music scene of that time – which Fujiwara is credited with introducing to Tokyo, and an extremely cool imaginary band called Louis V and The Fragments. It featured preppy elements, and items ranged from clothing and accessories (hats, a retro multicoloured iridescent carabiner) to bags and backpacks (in Monogram Canvas and Monogram Eclipse, with some of the pieces reading 'Louis Vuitton Paris Fragment'). There was also a Monogram teddy bear and even, most fittingly, a guitar case in Monogram Eclipse.

ANNIVERSARY EDITIONS

Anniversaries have always been a great way to celebrate a brand's heritage and, in the case of Louis Vuitton, this has often been achieved by inviting creatives belonging to different arenas to collaborate and produce something extraordinary. For the iconic Monogram's 160th birthday, for instance, a limited-edition book, *Louis Vuitton: The Icon and the Iconoclasts: A Celebration of Monogram*, showing sketches, images and insight into the project's inspirations, accompanied a unique collection of pieces created by cherry-picked designers. And for the founder's bicentenary, there was something for everybody: a book, a documentary, an exhibition and even an NFT game for the more techie fashionistas. Such events not only support Louis Vuitton's commitment to their savoir faire but also reflect their entrepreneurial vision and innovation, bringing together different platforms and attracting diverse audiences in the process.

100th Anniversary of the Monogram Canvas

To mark the centenary of the Monogram in 1996, the Maison invited six fashion designers to create unique pieces of luggage. This quirky collection showcased interpretations by Helmut Lang, who created a DJ's vinyl box; Sybilla, who designed a backpack with a matching built-in umbrella; a pointed hiking bag by Romeo Gigli; Manolo Blahnik's oval shoe trunk; and Vivienne Westwood's 'bustle bag' – to be worn at the small of the back, held by the hand, or hung from the shoulder. The collection was exhibited globally – celebrating, once again, the brand's creative and adventurous ethos.

Opposite: A huge Louis Vuitton suitcase outside the Plaza 66 shopping mall in Shanghai, China. The woman carries the Manhattan bag in Monogram canvas.

Iconoclasts Collection

Under the auspices of Nicolas Ghesquière, who joined Louis Vuitton as Artistic Director of womenswear in 2013, the following year the Maison asked six designers to put their mark on the iconic Monogram to celebrate its 160th anniversary. Limited editions were created by the chosen team who, once again, came up with something both unique and personal. The French fashion designer Christian Louboutin created a bag and a matching shopping trolley, both featuring a red panel and trim, reminiscent of his legendary, red-lacquered stiletto soles. Artist and photographer Cindy Sherman made a camera bag and a vanity trunk with 31 coloured drawers (in different shades of green, yellow and blue) and travel stamps from made-up places, called Studio in a trunk, complete with a foldable stool and a mirror. Canadian–American architect Frank Gehry designed a rectangular box that looked like it was twisted. It had a detachable shoulder strap, a golden clasp to close it, and a lining of blue lambskin embossed with the LV logo. The legendary Karl Lagerfeld, who photographed the lookbook for this venture, came up with a boxing collection: a trunk and a punching bag, which came in three sizes: baby, PM and GM, with a pair of matching boxing gloves. The trunk had four removable shelves, a mat and an optional stand with 12 Monogram weights. Marc Newson designed a Monogram canvas and a shearling backpack available in blue, beige or orange; and designer Rei Kawakubo, founder of Comme des Garçons (who had collaborated with the House in 2008), created a Sac Plat tote bag featuring three asymmetrical cut-out holes.

Opposite: As part of the 100th anniversary of the Monogram canvas, in 1996, Vivienne Westwood created a 'bustle bag', which could be worn with a strap, hand-held or positioned to sit at the small of one's back.

Above and opposite: *A brown Monogram twisted box designed by Frank Gehry (above) and Karl Lagerfeld's Monogram punchbag with matching boxing gloves, for the Iconoclasts collection in 2014 (opposite).*

Overleaf: *A giant Louis Vuitton trunk is displayed in Moscow's Red Square as part of the 'Soul of Adventures' exhibition in 2013.*

200th Anniversary of the Birth of Louis Vuitton

Milestone celebrations are a wonderful way of making history and an opportunity to create something special. As expected, the highly anticipated 200th birthday celebration for the founder was nothing short of spectacular, and took a number of different guises. Some stores (including Singapore's Island Maison at Marina Bay, Tokyo's Shibuya store and the Fifth Avenue flagship boutique in New York) were given a temporary facelift when covered with a pixelated, Damier-inspired print with a large drawing of M. Vuitton that read 'Happy Birthday Louis'. There was also an interactive game called Louis: The Game, available to download from his birthday that year

Above: *Former New York department store Barney's was painted for the exhibition 'Louis Vuitton's 200 Trunks, 200 Visionaries'.*

Opposite: *A grand total of 31,700 Lego bricks was used to create Louis Vuitton's Birthday Cake trunk, displayed at the exhibition celebrating his 200th birthday.*

– 4 August 2022 – and starring the House's mascot Vivienne, launched in 2018. Customers were invited to join her (a small, four-petalled doll with a quatrefoil patch over its right eye), as she travelled through multiple worlds, retracing the brand's history and collecting 200 birthday candles.

Also as part of the bicentenary, the House of Louis Vuitton invited 200 artists across diverse disciplines (from architects like Frank Gehry and Sou Fujimoto, to musicians like British DJ Benji B) to design a 50 × 50 × 100 cm (19⅔ × 19⅔ × 39⅓ in) trunk, a similar size to the very first flat-top version launched by Louis Vuitton when he started his business as a malletier in 1854. The exciting project was driven by Faye McLeod, Louis Vuitton's Visual Image Director, and Ansel Thompson, Senior Art Director, who 'wanted to explore the idea of the trunk as a blank canvas'. As explained by McLeod, 'These were then displayed in our global store windows, before being regrouped for "200 Trunks, 200 Visionaries: The Exhibition".' The show began in Asnières, Louis Vuitton's spiritual home. From there, it travelled to Singapore, then Los Angeles and finally to New York. A Sotheby's auction took place the following year, with all proceeds going to a Louis Vuitton scholarship programme.

While some of the thought-provoking and inspiring designs were physical, others were projections or digital interpretations, but collectively this extraordinary exhibition conveyed the brand's spirit of adventure. An example was the 'container of ideas' by designer Pierre Yovanovitch, a colour-block rendition that 'pays homage to the trunk as a container of nostalgia, creativity, and emotion.' Architect Peter Marino covered his in tight-fitting black leather straps, a reference to Houdini's successful underwater trunk escape in 1912 (albeit not from a Louis Vuitton trunk). Hannes Peer had his trunk covered in a travel-sticker collage, the astrologer Susan Miller devised M. Vuitton's astrological birth chart, from which the brand's design team created a model of the planetary alignment inside her trunk. On the main level of the exhibition. there was even a Jukebox trunk designed by British DJ Benji B, with a curated playlist of 200 tracks that played on a loop. Some rooms were dedicated to individual designers, including Frank Gehry, who created 'a tea party for Louis', and Robert Moy's Brooklyn Balloon Company, whose colourful balloon-covered trunk in a balloon-filled room created an immersive experience. 'The vessel-shaped sculpture is made from 122 inflated latex balloons dripped in 14 coats of epoxy; then sanded, and polished to a high gloss; and finally brush painted,' the designer explained.

Louis Vuitton's luggage – the trunk in particular – continues to be a source of inspiration and a canvas of expression for artists worldwide. And with creativity being at the heart of the brand, as

Above: *Architect Peter Marino designed the Houdini trunk, on display at Louis Vuitton's '200 Trunks, 200 Visionaries' exhibition (top). Virgil Abloh collaborated with Louis Vuitton to create the striking Monogram Eclipse Rainbow collection (bottom).*

Above: *Jean-Michel Othonel's India-themed trunk, made from glass bricks, featured in the Louis Vuitton 200th anniversary exhibition.*

stated by Faye McLeod, limited-edition pieces keep on delighting Louis Vuitton fans and collectors alike. And there is always something for everyone: from Virgil Abloh's Spring/Summer 2019 black rainbow Monogram Malle Courrier with black hardware (Abloh was Artistic Director of Louis Vuitton's menswear line, with collections from 2018–21), or his colourful, graffiti-inspired design for Spring/Summer 2021, to contemporary artist Grayson Perry's LVAM1 (Louis Vuitton Alan Measles 1) in 2022, the choice is extensive. Perry's bespoke trunk was made to coincide with his exhibition 'The Tomb of the Unknown Craftsman', which took place at the British Museum. This beautiful shrine to his teddy bear, Alan Measles, is adorned with the folkloric figures Perry has become known for – although the bear on display was in fact Elton, Alan's 'stunt double'. Always maintaining functionality at heart, this piece – which was also shown at the Exhibition Space in the New Bond Street store – was designed to transport the artist's flamboyant dresses to the Venice Biennale the following year.

Below: Willo Perron's metal trunk, created for the '200 Trunks, 200 Visionaries' exhibition, is a motorized futuristic idea of a trunk that will move and unpack itself.

CHAPTER

4

CELEBRITIES & OTHER STORIES

'There's a lot of baggage that comes along with our family, but it's like Louis Vuitton baggage.'

Kim Kardashian,
businesswoman and social-media star

A-LIST CLIENTS

Since its inception in 1854, Louis Vuitton has always maintained an A-list client base. It has included explorers, writers, royalty, the entertainment elite and numerous celebrities around the world – from Jackie Kennedy to the Kardashians.

Perhaps one of the brand's greatest strengths has been the ability to retain its premium quality and identity while adjusting to a changing world of travel, fashion and social trends – from the very early trunks to those made during the Belle Époque, and the travel bags that emerged throughout the Roaring Twenties (Sac Marin 1927) and beyond (Speedy and Keepall 1930, Noé 1932). As independent post-war women joined the workforce in earnest, bags and handbags became objects of desire, and men too required briefcases, suitcases and wallets, which needed to be stylish as well as practical. All of these were provided by the House.

During the 1950s and 1960s, the brand began to appear on the arms of numerous jet-setting stars, which made the luggage a symbol of luxury status that became synonymous with its excellence and heritage. Actresses Juliette Gréco and Catherine Deneuve, as well as the latter's then husband, fashion photographer David Bailey, were spotted carrying them, as was the Italian actress Anna Magnani, who was famously snapped in Paris in 1960 next to her Louis Vuitton luggage collection. Brigitte Bardot was another celebrity who effortlessly endorsed the brand, alongside Hollywood names such as Audrey Hepburn, who requested a personalized Speedy made in a 25 cm (10 in) length, a version that still forms part of the collection

Opposite: Scarlett Johansson is photographed by Mert and Marcus for Louis Vuitton's Autumn/Winter 2007 campaign, holding a Monogram Mirage Griet bag.

today, and Lauren Bacall, whose initialled luggage collection was sold at auction for $37,000 in 2015. Louis Vuitton was now recognized the world over, featured regularly in fashion magazines, such as *Vogue* and *Harper's Bazaar*, and was fast becoming hugely aspirational. The fashion landscape developed through the next decades – the Swinging Sixties, power dressing in the 1980s – but it wasn't until 1997, when Vuitton appointed Marc Jacobs as Artistic Director, that a new energy was injected into the Maison, something that would shape its future.

Above: *Catherine Deneuve and her husband David Bailey arrive at London Airport in 1966.*

Opposite: *Audrey Hepburn with a Louis Vuitton Speedy in Rome's airport, 1968.*

The New Millennium

Under Jacobs, as the brand took a new direction, so did its celebrity following. Louis Vuitton were pioneers in combining art and fashion, which appealed to a large audience – an audience that could now be reached through the new social media platforms and other technological advances. Launched in 2007 and continued until 2012, an advertising campaign called Core Values became a snapshot of the House's heritage. It featured a number of striking portraits of celebrities with their Louis Vuitton luggage, taken by Annie Leibovitz. These included Angelina Jolie, who was photographed barefoot in a small wooden boat carrying a Monogram tote (near the Siem Reap province of Cambodia, where Maddox, her eldest son, was adopted) Sean Connery next to his waterproof Keepall, leaning on the wooden dock near his Bahamas residence (a shot that was, in fact, a test before the actor went into hair and make-up); and Catherine Deneuve photographed at a Paris train station sitting elegantly on a suitcase with a steam train in the background – the tagline reading 'Sometimes, home is just a feeling'. Further campaigns have included Steven Meisel's Spring/Summer 2009 shoot starring Madonna at the Café Figaro in Los Feliz, California, and Meisel's Autumn/Winter 2010 campaign, with models Natalia Vodianova, Christy Turlington and Karen Elson together in a 1950s-style backstage changing room, complete with classic light-bulb mirrors.

Jacobs's final campaign for Louis Vuitton, for Spring/Summer 2014, was a series of portraits of his muses Fan Bingbing, Sofia Coppola, Gisele Bündchen, Catherine Deneuve, Caroline de Maigret and Edie Campbell, also photographed by Steven Meisel. They all carry a limited edition of the Noé bag, originally designed by Gaston-Louis Vuitton in 1932 to hold champagne bottles, called NN14.

Above: *Catherine Deneuve holding a Manhattan Monogram bag while sitting on Louis Vuitton luggage in a 2007 advert with the strapline 'Sometimes home is just a feeling'.*

Overleaf: *Angelina Jolie photographed by Annie Leibovitz for the Louis Vuitton Core Values campaign, carrying her own monogrammed Alto bag.*

The 2010s and Beyond

Since Nicolas Ghesquière took the helm as Creative Director in 2013, the House's ambassadors have reflected his views and ideas. His first advertising campaign for Autumn/Winter 2014, entitled Series 1, brought together the work of photographers Annie Leibovitz, Juergen Teller and Bruce Weber, providing a fresh individual vision for Louis Vuitton from three very different standpoints. 'I wanted an unprecedented narrative from each of these photographers whom I admire so greatly,' said Ghesquière. Bruce Weber selected models Liya Kebede, Jean Campbell and Kirstin Liljegren and photographed them in Miami; Juergen Teller captured model Freja Beha at the Venice Biennale and Annie Leibovitz shot Charlotte Gainsbourg in New York.

Right: *Kate Moss photographed with a perforated Musette bag for the Spring/Summer 2006 campaign.*

Other timeless photoshoots include the 2023 campaign with actress Zendaya (as the face of the iconic Capucines bag designed in 2013), shot by duo Mert and Marcus in France's Côte d'Azur and Horizons Never End, photographed by Glen Luchford in 2023, which celebrated the spirit of travel, showcasing the Horizon suitcase collection designed by Marc Newson. Here, model Gisele Bündchen is on a Miami beach, singer and producer Jackson Wang is in Paris at dawn, and footballer Lionel Messi is seen at an airport terminal — each with their respective luggage.

As captain of the Argentinian football team, in 2022 Messi received the FIFA World Cup trophy (made of 18-carat gold and malachite and weighing 6.175 kg/13 2/3 lb) in a bespoke Louis Vuitton

Opposite: *Lionel Messi was photographed by Glen Luchford for the Horizons Never End campaign, 2023.*

Left: *The 2018 FIFA World Cup trophy was transported in a custom-made Louis Vuitton trunk.*

Malles Trophée, created in Asnières by master artisans. Louis Vuitton had designed these trunks for the World Cup in 2010, 2014 and 2018. Interestingly, the 2018 World Cup trunk, featured in the Louis Vuitton campaign, was shot by Annie Leibovitz and released the day before the 2022 FIFA World Cup competition began. It shows Lionel Messi with rival Cristiano Ronaldo playing chess on Damier chequerboard. The chess pieces were positioned to recreate a legendary game between grandmasters Magnus Carlsen and Hikaru Nakamura. The game ended in a draw.

Other trophy trunks include one for the Formula 1 Grand Prix de Monaco and one for the Davis Cup tennis competition (commissioned in 2019). This was a striking circular Trophy travel case covered in the Monogram Macassar canvas (a dark print based on the hazel and black stripes found on Macassar ebony wood). Louis Vuitton also produced a trunk for the America's Cup, made by hand by three craftsmen, who worked for over 400 hours to complete it.

An Exciting Appointment

Having collaborated with the house in 2004 and 2008, record producer and recording artist Pharrell Williams joined Louis Vuitton in 2023 as their menswear Creative Director, a controversial appointment to replace the late Virgil Abloh. Williams's Spring/Summer 2024 debut collection was staged on the Pont Neuf in Paris, the city's oldest bridge, and was a huge spectacle that went beyond a traditional fashion show. As described by Osman Ahmed, Fashion Features Director at i-D magazine, 'It's the convergence between entertainment and fashion, and mass appeal and luxury.' He added, 'I think it is going to be one of those moments when we look back and [see it] as a turning point.'

Putting his personal stamp on a debut collection that was bursting with streetwear and contemporary tailoring, Williams created the Damoflage print, which brought the traditional Damier check and a camouflage colour palette together. It was everywhere, from accessories through to denim and tailoring – even on a series of stacked trunks that made their way onto the runway on a golf buggy driven by one of the models. On the front row, a long list of celebrities supported the designer: Jay-Z (who opened the after-party), Beyoncé, Maluma, A$AP Rocky, Zendaya, Lewis Hamilton, Kelly Rowland, Tyler, the Creator, Kim Kardashian – and, of course, Rihanna, who starred in the Spring/Summer 2024 advertising campaign. In the images, she is seen showing her baby bump while holding a take-away hot drink and carrying some LV luggage in bright yellow, red and emerald green – now made of super-soft leather and screen-printed, instead of the traditional canvas.

Above: *Pharrell Williams' s debut show as Creative Director of menswear for Louis Vuitton, Spring/Summer 2024, took place on the Pont Neuf in Paris and included a collection of trunks and plenty of smaller luggage.*

Overleaf: *Pharrell Williams's personal vision and adaptation of the legendary Damier motif ranged from accessories to clothing.*

Above: Naomi Campbell stands with a dog and her designer Louis Vuitton luggage collection at the Dorchester Hotel in London.

Opposite: Elle Fanning arriving at Nice ariport, carrying her customized Keepall, in 2019.

CINEMATIC APPEARANCES

Given that Louis Vuitton luggage is an emblem of the golden age of travel and a firm status symbol, it is no surprise that it regularly features in films and TV series, from James Bond's classic *A View to a Kill* (1985), in which Roger Moore played a wealthy heir travelling with an extensive Louis Vuitton collection, to *Barbie* (2023), starring Margot Robbie, in which an iridescent PVC Monogram Keepall Bandoulière 50 is spotted in Barbie's wardrobe.

Some early Hollywood films, such as the romantic comedy *Love in the Afternoon* (1957), starring Audrey Hepburn and Gary Cooper, show key pieces – in this instance a Louis Vuitton Wardrobe trunk in the corridor of the Ritz Hotel in Paris. *Charade* (1963), another light-hearted movie starring Audrey Hepburn, this time with Cary Grant, also shows some LV suitcases. Hepburn, as Regina Lampert, carries her belongings around in a valise set and a Monogram Steamer bag.

Left: A Wardrobe trunk is seen in Love in the Afternoon *(1957), featuring Audrey Hepburn and Gary Cooper.*

Opposite: *Bob Hope and Anita Ekberg starring in* Paris Holiday *(1958), with a Louis Vuitton Monogram Wardrobe trunk and a matching vanity case.*

In the drama *Titanic* (1997), set in 1912, we see a further display of beautiful Louis Vuitton luggage collections that includes vanity cases, suitcases and large trunks that would have belonged to passengers of the time. Another display of Louis Vuitton luggage is seen in the movie *Coming to America* (1988), a comedy in which Prince Akeem, played by Eddie Murphy, travels to the USA and goes undercover to find true love, taking with him numerous monogrammed Louis Vuitton trunks and suitcases to accommodate his royal wardrobe. *The Talented Mr. Ripley* (1999), starring Jude Law, Matt Damon, Gwyneth Paltrow and Cate Blanchett, is another cinematic production in which LV luggage plays an integral part of the film's overall aesthetic.

Above: Paris Hilton in Episode 11 of Saturday Night Live, 2005, with a white Louis Vuitton Multicolore Speedy, designed by Japanese artist Takashi Murakami.

Wes Anderson's *The Darjeeling Limited* (2007) is a memorable picture that tells the story of three brothers who are reunited, a year after the death of their father, on a train trip to India to visit their mother in a convent. The monogrammed luggage set for this feature was a collaboration between Marc Jacobs and Wes's brother Eric Chase Anderson, and had animals and trees as well as initials and numbers on the bags. The pieces were symbolic of the characters' emotional load and became a talking point amongst critics. Some have even described them as the real stars of the show.

Further examples include *Catch Me If You Can* (2002), in which Leonardo DiCaprio, as Frank Abagnale Jr, holds a Monogram suitcase full of cash; the musical drama Nine (2009), which displays a stacked set of Monogram luggage, complete with a hat box (when Penelope Cruz as Carla Albanese travels on the train) and *Blue Jasmine* (2013), the story of Jasmine, a socialite played by Cate Blanchett, who falls on hard times. A feast for the eyes.

Left: Chris Noth on location for Annie Leibowitz's Sex and the City *photoshoot for* Vogue *magazine, carrying Louis Vuitton luggage.*

Overleaf: In The Darjeeling Limited *(2007), three brothers carry suitcases that had belonged to their father. The pieces were a collaboration between the then Artistic Director Marc Jacobs and Eric Chase Anderson.*

CHAPTER

5

CRAFTSMANSHIP & CARE

'Don't expect me to advise you to travel with ugly luggage just because you're afraid it will get stolen.'

Patrick-Louis Vuitton,
great-great-grandson of the brand's founder

QUALITY MATERIALS

The unique materials traditionally used over generations by Louis Vuitton to create their luggage have played a huge part in the brand's success. Never compromising on quality, these were adapted not only to developments in the travel industry, but also to answer new aesthetic demands from travellers worldwide.

The main material used when making a trunk is, of course, wood, and Louis Vuitton favoured sturdy poplar wood for its lightness and flexibility. Historically, it was sourced and transported up the River Seine to arrive at Vuitton's Asnière's workshop, where it was prepared and cut into strips. Today, poplar is still used by the house (30-year-old wood, which is dried for at least four years) to create the frames, as well as African okoume plywood (used on the lid and the body of the trunk), which shares many of poplar's characteristics, and is regularly used when manufacturing yachts and other vehicles requiring a lightweight base. The decorative, darker slats that sit across the trunk, however, are usually made of beechwood.

Another interesting material used by Louis Vuitton, often mistaken for leather, is lozine, a type of vulcanized cardboard, that is particularly rigid and durable and doesn't rot. It's also lighter than leather, making it a suitable choice, and the ideal protective material. When hammering the lozine into the edges of a trunk, thousands of nails may be required. Sometimes vegetable-tanned leather was also used when making a trunk, but never to reinforce its edges. This type of skin was specifically selected because it was considered luxurious, and developed a natural patina over time that got darker with age. This variant is still used today and is a very light beige when new.

Opposite: Virgil Abloh's menswear Autumn/Winter 2021 collection featured oversized coats and lots of luggage.

Brass is another signature material used by the Maison – on locks, clasps and nails – that can be polished when restored, to return it to its former glory. And remember, Louis Vuitton locks have a single key, handmade for each customer, which will open all of their luggage. Other metals used to make trunks were zinc and copper, especially on Explorer trunks, because it protected their contents from the unpredictable elements, insects and wildlife.

The use of exceptional canvas coverings is something that today still sets Louis Vuitton apart from any other luggage-maker. Designed in 1896, the Monogram was first made of a two-tone cotton jacquard material, which was coated in varnish. Over time this wore off, leaving the fabric exposed and vulnerable. Pieces with this finish that are still in circulation today are often tired-looking, but should you come across an original, remember that these are true gems, and are highly sought-after by collectors worldwide. In 1904, the pattern was hand-painted onto a treated canvas with a waxed, stencilled finish. This is why, despite its uniformity, there are small discrepancies within the design, adding to its character. In 1959, technological developments and a new coating process resulted in a more supple PVC canvas finish, which could be used on smaller items such as bags and wallets. It was a printed canvas with a cotton backing that was completely waterproof. Monogram prints from this time and beyond will be perfectly symmetrical and its motifs identical, row after row.

Opposite: Suitcases in the workshops of Louis Vuitton at Asnières, France, in 2021.

THE MAKING OF A LUXURY TRUNK

While some materials employed by the House of Louis Vuitton may have evolved to adapt to new technologies, when making luggage, the traditional craftsmanship and age-old methodologies used have seen little change since M. Vuitton launched his business in 1854. The workshop in Asnières, which currently employs close to 200 staff, has a studio flooded with natural light, complete with additional state-of-the-art overhead lighting to allow every last detail to be observed. It creates approximately 350 pieces each year – some emblematic classic pieces, and some special orders in rare and exotic leathers. Creating an off-the-shelf Wardrobe trunk will take the atelier's craftsmen and women approximately 150 hours to complete, using 400 metal pieces and around 4 m (13 ft) of canvas. A bespoke service is available too, for those who wish – and can afford – to put

Above: A trunk in the making: the Monogram canvas in being applied in the workshop.

their own stamp on a precious custom-built piece. This process starts with a watercolour impression of the design, which is then made into a 3D mock-up, featuring the customer's choice of covering materials, interior linings and configurations, and takes between six and eight months to complete.

As with any craft, the making of an exceptional trunk takes place in stages, and requires incredible dedication, care and, above all, skill. Aged poplar wood is primarily used by Vuitton for the wooden frames, as well as okoume and beech (as mentioned earlier), all of which are light as well as durable. A precious Louis Vuitton × Yayoi Kusama Flaconnier (bottle carrier), for example, begins its life as a poplar frame. Once the box is ready, textile reinforcement is applied throughout the interior, with extraordinary precision. With the aid of a thick paintbrush, the inside of the box is completely prepped with a coat of adhesive and then lined with strips of cotton fabric, which are cut to size and strategically placed onto the wooden surface to strengthen it. Sometimes, further insulation will be provided by adding zinc sheeting on the base. Some of the hinges on a Louis Vuitton trunk are made of cotton that is stitched together and then glued to the inside of the frame – a method that hasn't changed since Monsieur Vuitton opened his first shop.

Left: A Louis Vuitton travel case in Damier Azure canvas at the factory in Asnières in 2010.

To upholster the exterior, a small roller is sometimes used to prime both the wood and the canvas, and any other finish requested. The artisan will then cover the wood with the fabric, which will have been cut to size previously so that it lines up to perfection with every seam and joint – legend has it that the artisan will first sign the trunk with a hidden stamp. The fabric is then positioned onto the wood and pressed down meticulously. Once in place, it is blow-dried; any excess material is cut by hand with scissors and later trimmed with a scalpel. Some canvases, such as the Yayoi Kusama × Louis Vuitton limited edition, are customized with precious artwork. For Kusama's collaboration in 2023, a multi-step, screen-printing technique called serigraphy was applied by layers and by colour, recreating the artist's joyful, hand-painted pattern. It was then embossed to create 3D relief on the individual polka dots.

Once the canvas is in place, most trunks will have the edges protected with strips of lozine. The vulcanized fibre is nailed along the edges to protect and reinforce the trunk. Any interior shelving or compartments will have been created separately by expert carpenters, and at this stage will be covered in the selected finish before being positioned inside the vessel. In the case of the Yayoi Kusama × Louis Vuitton trunk, Vuittonite was used – the vinyl-like material that was used to cover the interior of luggage and bags prior to 1997. If the inside of the lid is quilted and cushioned to protect its contents, this will also be done separately, and ribbon will be added to it before it is placed and secured onto the main lid using glue and nails.

The trunk is then taken to a different station, where the hardware is applied. Brass brackets are placed on the sides and corners, and hammered in by hand with matching brass nails, to reinforce the piece and protect it from any shock exposure. The personalized multi-tumbler lock from the 1980s is also fixed on at this stage, using a drill and nails. And finally, if the item of luggage has a handle, it will be nailed in. With the brassware fixed, any inside compartments can now be slotted into place with a hammer, as in the limited-edition LV × Yayoi Kusama trunk, which has a secret drawer and is designed to carry three perfume bottles.

It is now time to apply any finishing touches such as vachetta leather pull tabs on any drawers, which are tinted on the sides with a thin paintbrush to create definition and then hammered into place. For the Louis Vuitton × Yayoi Kusama collaboration, a specially designed stitched badge was carefully glued onto the Vuittonite, using a template to place it exactly in the centre and provide the perfect embellishment. Sometimes a saddle stitch is used for such detailing, using two needles and a wax-coated thread. On other occasions, machine stitching will be favoured for its uniformity. To ensure flawlessness, the trunk is smoothed and checked for any imperfections. After inspection it will be ready to be sold and embark on a brand new journey.

Left: A side handle with gold hardware and 'Louis Vuitton Paris' embossed in the leather.

HALLMARKS OF AUTHENTICITY

When shopping for Louis Vuitton luggage, preloved luxury outlets can be a great starting point. You may be a collector searching for pieces with a bit of history, a discontinued case you've set your heart on, or perhaps simply a bargain. It can be fun searching in markets, antique stores and online for that special something. You may also be able to pick up an exceptional item at a respectable auction house. But beware, Louis Vuitton's quintessential style has attracted counterfeits dating back to the nineteenth century. As a response, Louis and his son Georges first designed and trademarked the Damier print (1888), followed by the Monogram (1896). This didn't stop fakes, however, from replicas by Harlem designer Dapper Dan (Daniel Day), who appropriated Vuitton's prints and used them in his own line of clothing and accessories in the 1980s and 90s, to the surge of the 'superfakes', which are sold as both new and second-hand items. Many of these are advertised online, with one statistic showing that a staggering 95 per cent of listings classified as Louis Vuitton are either fake, or the item sent to the customer will be.

But there are some pointers that will help you identify the genuine article and, if in doubt, you can always have your items authenticated by a vintage expert. Remember that Louis Vuitton never discount their items, and if the luggage you're after is still in production, it's always a good idea to have a look at the Louis Vuitton catalogue and study every last detail – such as the positioning of the canvas, which is invariably consistent. The logo on a Neverfull Damier canvas Grande Modèle bag, for example, will always be on the sixth square from the top. Read on to find out what to look out for when searching for that hidden treasure.

Above: *Louis Vuitton suitcases for sale at Portobello Market in London.*

1. Overall Impression

As a premium brand, Louis Vuitton will only ever source the best materials available on the market, and all items – from suitcases to satchels – will be manufactured with the utmost care. The smell and buttery feel of the leather, the symmetry, the precise alignment of the canvas and the weight of the hardware are all elements that will bring any genuine piece to life. A legendary trunk, for instance, will always have a defining border made of lozine with brass corners, a central lock and – if large enough – clasps on either side. While there may be rips on the coverings or missing brackets on a trunk, the pattern shouldn't completely fade with time, and the craftsmanship, quality and structure of an original item should always shine through. Interestingly, Louis Vuitton made his trunks based on the ancient golden ratio, also known as the 'divine proportion', as observed in nature. It's a mathematical formula that has been widely used in art, first discovered by Euclid around 300 BCE, and possibly the reason Vuitton's luggage is so pleasing to the eye.

2. Check the Alignment

Some of the most copied items from the luggage collection are the vanity boxes, which haven't changed since they were first designed, and the bottle carrier, or flaconnier. Larger fake trunks are in the minority, and usually easily spotted if counterfeit. One way to establish if a piece is genuine is to look at the alignment of the covering. A genuine Vuitton design will always have its prints perfectly straight, and the print will follow on any flaps or lids, a painstakingly precise process. You will never come across an angled or off-centre print, and it will always be parallel to the edges.

In the case of the Monogram, there are three motifs that are repeated diagonally in the same order throughout, ad infinitum (a fleur-de-lis, a circle, another fleur-de-lis and the LV logo), and the LV insignia is very rarely cut off (as opposed to the other emblems). Some hand luggage, for example the Speedy, is made from a single piece of canvas, fabric or leather (with the exception of some early versions where two pieces meet on the base). So if the bag is genuine and has a pattern, it will follow one direction all the way through, and on one side it will be inverted. Aside from some of their collaborations, such as Stephen Sprouse's Monogram roses (2009), which are scattered on the canvas, even the initials on a personalized item will be centred in relation to its height and length, creating a sense of overall balance.

3. Inspect the Leather

Traditionally, Louis Vuitton have used vegetable-tanned cowhide (not treated) or vachetta leather, because it is particularly soft. Sometimes it is used to make an entire handbag or piece of hand luggage, but it is mostly seen on handles, straps and pull tags. Untreated vachetta is a particular skin that oxidizes when in contact with UV rays and absorbs any oils it comes into contact with when handled, which causes it gradually to darken over time, creating a beautiful patina. If you can identify the date your item was created, you can then work out how dark it should be (from a light honey tone to a golden-brown amber), which can confirm its legitimacy. Of course, the item may have been preserved away from the light, but overall, a vintage item will have dark leather (a caramel shade). If it's fake and leatherette has been used instead, it won't change colour and will look and feel almost plastic to the touch.

4. Consider the Stitching

Unless your luggage is part of a limited-edition series, or produced with an updated version of the original canvas, if it has stitching on untreated vachetta leather (on straps, handles or pull tabs) this will be clean and crisp and assembled using yellow thread (a shade close to mustard colour) and sometimes brown. Darker leathers will have darker threads to match. The stitching will be completely uniform and symmetrical (the number of stitches on either side of a bag, for instance, should match) with no missed or loose stitches in sight. The majority of sewing is machine-made, but there are examples, such as the Steamer bag, where some seams are hand-sewn, which is why this bag is very rarely copied.

5. Feel the Hardware

The majority of Louis Vuitton's original luggage range has solid brass hardware that feels heavy when held. Although it may show signs of wear and tear, and may sometimes have developed a coating, when polished it should gleam and show no dullness or a brushed finish. Some more recent models and limited-edition pieces may utilize other metals, for example ruthenium (on Eclipse Monogram-covered trunks).

RIVETS AND STUDS All rivets and studs used will have either 'Louis Vuitton' or 'LV' embossed on them, unless they are too small to accommodate any stamping – as is the case for the nails holding down the lozine border.

ZIPS Checking the zipper can tell you a lot about an item. On a Louis Vuitton travel bag, a zip will always be smooth and glide seamlessly when pulled. Its appearance can also provide a guide when determining when it was made, and ascertaining whether or not it is authentic. To keep up with demand, from the 1970s until the early 1990s Louis Vuitton worked with a US agency called The French Company through a licensing agreement. Items sold by this third party used a variety of zips (Talon, Éclair, Robin, Coats & Clarks), some which are shiny and others matte. After 1991, Louis Vuitton manufactured all their own gold brass hardware, featuring the LV logo.

LOCKS While the very first trunks made by Louis Vuitton had two locks and were reinforced by a leather strap, from 1886 onwards a single central lock was used. With clasps on either side, a genuine Louis Vuitton lock will be made of solid brass and won't be plated. It will also be stamped with 'Louis Vuitton', the address where it was constructed (1 Rue Scribe Paris, 289 Oxford Street London or

454 Strand London) and a number, which will match a reference inside the trunk corresponding to the key – in case this was lost and a replacement was required. And although there may be some natural wear and tear, the details and finish should still be of a high quality.

Some luggage items have a double-push 'S' lock, like the one originally designed in 1910. It offered easy access to trunk boxes and suitcases, as the lock stays in place while the left bolt moves towards the centre when opening it. A magnetic-closure modern version is also available on some of the more recent Louis Vuitton items. Your luggage may also come with a padlock. To authenticate it, look for a defined 'LV' logo on the front; on the back it will have a registered mark and read 'Louis Vuitton' plus either 'Paris', 'Made in France' or 'Paris Made in France'. On the base there will be a number that corresponds to the key.

Left: Louis Vuitton's locks, which were patented in 1890, have become legendary.

6. Check the Labels

There will usually be a paper or leather label inside a Louis Vuitton trunk with a number that will match the one stamped onto the lock. Sometimes, in luggage and small leather goods, a stitched-in leather label might be used, or the interior leather lining may have been hot-stamped (not printed) with 'LOUIS VUITTON PARIS'. Always in capitals, the 'L' has a short tail, the 'O' is circular and the double 'T's are very close together. 'Made in France' will be written in lower case, including the 'm'.

You may also come across a letter 'P' stamped over the label. This indicates that the bag was gifted to a lucky press or media member.

Above: An early Louis Vuitton label, attached to the interior of a trunk.

7. Understand Date Codes

During the 1980s, in an attempt to discourage copies, Louis Vuitton introduced date codes on their smaller pieces of luggage and handbags. Of course, these can be plagiarized, and codes can rub off or be lost when linings are replaced. While they don't guarantee that your piece is genuine, they can be very informative when researching your future investment. The date codes have changed over time. During the early 1980s, three or four numbers would represent the year (the first two) and month (the last one or two) in which the item was made. Later that decade, the same numbers were followed by two letters representing the manufacturer's location. The letters were also seen in front of the numbers in some of these bags. Between 1990 and 2006, the code was altered again: it had two letters representing the factory location, followed by four numbers. The first and third of these last four digits represented the month the item was made, and the second and fourth stood for the year of manufacture. And from 2007 until 2021, the two letters were still shorthand for the factory the bag was made in, but the first and third digits now determined the week in which a piece was made, and the second and fourth numbers, the year. There are many guides online that will help you decipher your Louis Vuitton date code. These codes can be found tucked away in different sections of the bag, depending on the model – sometimes behind a pocket or on a leather tab.

In March 2021, the date codes were replaced with microchip identification, with items now including RDFI (radio frequency identification) technology. These are concealed inside the bag, embedded in the lining and are encrypted with basic information about the products (the material used, the product reference, the date and place where it was manufactured). The microchips can't be modified and can only be scanned at a Louis Vuitton boutique.

CARING FOR YOUR LOUIS VUITTON

Looking after your precious Louis Vuitton luggage is easier than you think. Here are some dos and don'ts to remember.

When handling the leather, remember to avoid contact with alcohol-based products, including hand sanitizers, cleaning products, cosmetics and fragrances, as these may damage it. Depending on the leather, different cleaning methods are recommended by Louis Vuitton in their own product care information. Natural leather (vegetable-tanned cowhide leather) is untreated, and as such is very easily marked and scratched, but over time it develops a beautiful patina that enhances the product and adds to its charm and individuality. If the leather accidentally gets wet, make sure you blot it as soon as possible with a white, lint-free or soft microfibre cloth to absorb the liquid. Its delicate appearance is part of its allure and although it marks and scratches easily, over time the skin will darken, developing a unique identity.

If you need to clean calfskin or cowhide, always use a damp cloth (using only water) to wipe it clean. As this leather is of a very high standard, avoid using substances such as mink oil, alcohol-based products or other commercial cleaning chemicals, as it might age prematurely. It may have wrinkles or other natural imperfections, but as mentioned before, this only adds to the character of each individually crafted piece. Vernis leather, first seen in the Lous Vuitton Spring/Summer 1998 collection, is a variation with a shiny finish. Being more delicate, it is important to avoid direct sun exposure and contact with materials that may transfer their pigment onto the Vernis, such as magazines, other skins or denim.

For canvas finishes, once again, avoid contact with alcohol. Monogram and Damier canvas can be cleaned with a damp cloth and slightly soapy water, paying special attention to any layered printed areas. Highly pigmented materials can also transfer colour onto the canvas, so beware of contact with these, especially if your Louis Vuitton bag or trunk is one of the lighter editions (such as the Damier Azur), to help preserve the original pattern intact. If your canvas is printed it may fade in time, so it is suggested by Louis Vuitton that you rotate the use of your handbags.

If you're restoring a trunk, as well as gently wiping the canvas with soapy water, you will need to clean the inside. Depending on the material it has been lined with, you can use a damp cloth and a circular motion to remove any surface dirt. The brass can be safely cleaned too, and be brought back to its former glory. Use a specialist product and rub it a few times (using either a white cloth, paper towels or cotton buds), in a ventilated area, until shiny and clean.

Caring and cleaning for your items regularly will ensure they stay looking beautiful for longer and can continue to be your travel companions for many journeys and adventures to come.

Left: Louis Vuitton vintage leather-trimmed Monogram travel bag from the 1980s.

Overleaf: A red Épi leather Alma bag is held by a model next to a matching trunk, for the Louis Vuitton's Spring/Summer 2015 campaign.

INDEX

AUTHOR ACKNOWLEDGEMENTS

I'd like to thank my editor Lisa Dyer for her vision and inspiration; Siobhan Trewick from the vintage store Reboundstore.com for acting as consultant on this book; fashion designers Holger Auffenberg and Chris Mossom for their input and Natalia Farran and Lucia Graves for their feedback.

PICTURE CREDITS

The publishers would like to thank the following for their kind permission to reproduce the images in this book.

Special thanks: **Courtesy of Dumitru Tira – Pushkin Antiques/Alessio Lorenzi, www.pushkinantiques.com:** 19t, 25t, 25b, 37, 47, 49, 61, 62, 150.

Advertising Archives: 34, 38, 40, 81, 90–1, 98–9, 110, 116–7, 118–9, 154–5. **AKG Images:** 13; © Les Arts Décoratifs, Paris/Jean Tholance 18, 19b, 19br, 24, 26, 27, 41, 42, 44–5, 60; Van Ham/Saša Fuis, Köln 28, 31. **Alamy:** Archivio GBB 12; Associated Press 69, 124–5; DPA Picture Alliance 63; Everett Collection Inc. 113, 128, 129; Frederic Reglain 84; Goddard New Era 58; Grzegorz Czapski 4; Hemis 115; Imaginechina Limited 95; Jack Ludlam 127; M. Sobreira 145; MAXPPP 139, 140; MAXPPP/Franck Dubray 149; Patti McConville 83; Paul Kennedy 85; Retro AdArchives 57; RiskyWalls 51; Sergio Azenha 22; Sipa US 102, 105t; Thomas Dutour 10; Trinity Mirror / Mirrorpix 112; ZUMA Press, Inc. 96. **Bridgeman:** ©Christie's Images 17, 73; Everett Collection 132–3. **Getty Images:** Abaca Press 121; Andreas Rentz 29; Andrew H. Walker 74–5; Apic 15; Bassignac/Benainous 80; Bloomberg 21t, 21b, 123; Christian Vierig 7; Cindy Ord 38–9; Dimitrios Kambouris 70–1; Edward Berthelot 54, 93, 105b; Emmanuel Dunand 120; Francois Guillot 89; Gou Yige 50; Houston Chronicle/Hearst Newspapers 153; James Devaney 131; Marc Piasecki 126; Miami Herald 78–9; Michael Buckner 103, 106, 107; Miguel Medina 141, 143; NBC 130; Pascal Le Segretain 136; Peter White 30; Richard Baker 92; Streetstyleshooters 52; Udo Salters Photography 77; Victor Boyko 100–1; Victor Virgile 55; WWD 66, 86, 87. **Shutterstock:** Helen89 59.